A PORTRAIT OF
NEWCASTLE

TONY HOPKINS

HALSGROVE

First published in Great Britain in 2004

Frontispiece photograph: Almond and cherry-blossom, and the Tyne Bridge, from the Gateshead side of the river.

British Library Cataloguing-in-Publication Data
A CIP record for this title is available from the British Library

ISBN 1 84114 393 6

HALSGROVE
Halsgrove House
Lower Moor Way
Tiverton, Devon EX16 6SS
Tel: 01884 243242
Fax: 01884 243325
email: sales@halsgrove.com
website: www.halsgrove.com

Printed and bound by D'Auria Industrie Grafiche Spa, Italy

INTRODUCTION

There can be few more stirring sights, for visitors or home-comers, than arriving at Newcastle by train from the south and suddenly seeing the vista open of the Tyne and its renowned bridges. For once, you hope the train will stop a hundred yards short of the station and leave you on the King Edward's Bridge, looking east to the profile of the Castle Keep, the Baltic, the crowns of St Nicholas' Cathedral and the Civic Centre, and St James' Park football stadium. People arriving by road have a different but equally dramatic welcome, from the Angel of the North, the Metro Centre and the roadside ruins of Hadrian's Wall.

This really is a city of all ages. But not just one city, nor one community. Until 1974, Newcastle was part of Northumberland, while Gateshead, south of the river, was in County Durham. Today they are united with Sunderland, South Shields and Tynemouth in the Metropolitan County of Tyne and Wear. Thus there is scope for fudged boundaries. However, this book keeps things simple and does not stray far from Newcastle/Gateshead, with a bias to the north side of the river and the city's epicentre.

Newcastle has been a vibrant and vital settlement at least since Roman times. *Pons Aelius*, a bridge and fort at the start of the original Hadrian's Wall, lies at the foundation of the modern city. Over and beside this stands a Norman keep, and close-by are fragments of the medieval town walls which helped protect the settlement through the Border Wars. Shipbuilding and coal brought prosperity and expansion, and while the riverside was dirty and smelly, bustling and brash, the civic heart of the city centred on classical architecture and the elegant sweep of Grey Street and Grainger Town.

The mixture of grand buildings, green spaces, historic pubs and churches, a great river and a maritime outlook, helped give Newcastle/Gateshead a unique character. As did the regional culture and the ways of its people. In recent years, a revitalised Quayside has made the place the hub of contemporary art and music, and a successful football team, two universities and a thousand clubs and restaurants have kept its atmosphere lively and colourful, day and night.

The photographs in this book were taken over a period of three months, from late winter to early summer in 2004. Cities change all the time, and I felt the best way to catch Newcastle's spirit was in a single heartbeat. There is no special theme and no obvious order to the images, nor have I worried about omissions or boundaries. Newcastle and Gateshead, north and south of the Tyne, have different stories to tell, but my own approach has simply been to wander to and fro whenever subjects have suggested themselves.

The choice of material is based on what I have found exciting, beautiful or essential. Thus a gas-holder appears on the next page to an art gallery, and a flurry of aristocratic almond blossom opposite a street-wise patch of ragwort. People appear in all sorts of places, often as a background or a context. For me, Newcastle is sinew as well as stone. In previous books I have concentrated on the countryside and coast of the North East. This one helps to round off the story and sign it off.

Tony Hopkins, July, 2004

West from Swan Hunters' shipyards, with the ruins and rebuilt bathhouse of *Segedunum* Roman Fort.
The river is wide and deep only because of extensive dredging in the mid-nineteenth century.

Sentinels on the south bank of the Tyne at Hebburn.

Ship repair yards are still active along the Tyne, though the great battleship
days are long gone. Looking west over Wallsend Dry Docks.

Boats sheltering at the mouth of the Ouseburn as the tide ebbs.

The Tyne on one of its showpiece days, the University Boat Race, with crowds gathered along the Quayside and on the Millennium Bridge. The race takes place every May between local rivals Durham and Newcastle. Durham usually wins.

Looking across the still waters of the Tyne to the Gateshead shore. The square building beside the river is the Baltic, once a derelict warehouse but now the Centre for Contemporary Arts. Beyond this, in the middle of the picture, is the curved glass dome of the Sage, the new centre for music in the region.

A city profile of shifting styles. The reflection of All Saints' Church in
the shimmering Tyne adds a touch of Monet to the scene.

Late summer evening on Newcastle's Quayside, the Baltic framed by the arch of the Millennium Bridge.

Scudding clouds on a bright March morning. The Millennium Bridge, a unique and elegant footbridge designed to tilt as ships pass beneath, is known locally as the Blinking Eye. The navigable channel is about 30m wide, marked by pillars sunk into the river-bed.

Sunset reflecting from the underside of the Millennium Bridge arch.

A summer evening, upstream from the Quayside, with the city's bridges a jumble of coloured lights.

The Swing Bridge (built in 1876) and the High Level Bridge,
upstream from Sandhill.

A spring morning, looking west from the Gateshead side of the Tyne Bridge over the Swing Bridge to the Guildhall and Sandhill. This is one of the oldest parts of the city, developed on the site of *Pons Aelius*, the Roman bridge and fort established by Hadrian in AD 122. Most of the city lies at a higher level, as indicated by the High Level Bridge.

A dusting of snow on the Swing Bridge: late winter from the High Level Bridge.

Rush-hour on the bridges. Most of Newcastle's famous seven bridges were built as a response to a century of increased congestion, by road and rail. This compressed view, from the Millennium Bridge, includes (from east to west) Tyne Bridge, Swing Bridge, High Level Bridge, Queen Elizabeth II Bridge, King Edward's Bridge and Redheugh Bridge.

The Tyne was one of the busiest working waterways in Europe when coal was king.
The ship moored beneath the Tyne Bridge is the Tuxedo Princess – a floating night-club.

A fast road over the river; the A167 on the Gateshead side of the
Tyne Bridge. This bridge was the longest single-span bridge
in Britain when it opened in 1928.

Steel footings of the
Tyne Bridge's famous arch.

Sunday Market on the Quayside.
The birds over the river are kittiwakes,
sea-going gulls which usually nest on
cliff ledges but have settled for a river-
view from the Tyne Bridge's
concrete towers.

George Milligan has been saving souls in Newcastle for over fifty years.
Sunday mornings find him along the Quayside, where his own soul was saved.

Sunday Market on the Quayside. One of the oldest chartered markets in England, and still a popular family attraction on a sunny spring morning.

Rising tide, upstream from the High Level Bridge, from the south (Gateshead) side of the river.

Beneath the High Level Bridge, very early on a spring morning. The half-timbered building on the Newcastle side is the Cooperage, one of the oldest pubs in the city. Above this on the skyline is the red Turnbull Building, once a vast warehouse but now a collection of exclusive penthouse flats.

The very *art nouveau* Bridge Hotel, in the shadow
of the High Level Bridge.

Another perspective on the Bridge Hotel and the High Level Bridge, from the top of the Castle Keep. The ingenious double-decker bridge was designed by Robert Stephenson (son of George) and was opened by Queen Victoria in 1849.

The best that can be said about the King Edward's Railway Bridge is that it has worked perfectly
for nearly a hundred years. It was always intended to be functional rather than decorative.
Looking east to the city centre from the Redheugh Bridge.

Redheugh Bridge, on the riverside walkway at Skinnerburn Road.
The other six Tyne bridges are visible downstream.

Beneath the Redheugh Bridge, looking south-east to Gateshead on a summer evening.

The Copthorne Hotel, a pleasant stroll along the riverside and a popular lunch-time venue for live music.

Neptune keeping the pigeons at bay, on the roof of Neptune House – formerly the Fish Market and now offices.

A cold morning across the rooftops, towards the Guildhall and the river.

Merchants' town houses, four and five storeys high, opposite the Guildhall and a stone's-throw from the river. When they were built in the seventeenth century, these houses were intended to look modern, sophisticated and expensive.

FROM THE ABOVE WINDOW
ON NOV 18TH 1772
BESSY SURTEES DESCENDED AND ELOPED WITH
JOHN SCOTT LATER CREATED 1ST EARL OF ELDON
AND LORD CHANCELLOR OF ENGLAND

Plaque beneath one of the upper windows of
Bessie Surtees House on Sandhill. Proof that
rich merchants' daughters were as brave as
they were foolhardy.

Timber-framed frontage at Bessie Surtees House.

Derwentwater Chambers and the fly-over of the Tyne Bridge. There is a steep gradient from this riverside level to the city centre, either via flights of narrow steps ('chares') or up The Side and Dean Street to Grey Street.

Blackfriars – a cloister surviving from a medieval Dominican friary – founded in 1239 on a site beside the City Walls. The old refectory is now a coffee shop, and the grassy square is one of the best places to sit for a few minutes to escape the city's bustle.

The buildings around Blackfriars cloister-yard were bought by the city corporation after the Dissolution in 1544, then leased to guilds or 'mysteries' ('Skinners and Glovers', 'Tanners and Tailors' etc). In the last few years, Blackfriars has been renovated and the buildings leased again to local crafts and boutiques.

The Castle Keep and Black Gate. A wooden castle was built on a motte (mound) on this site in 1080 by Robert, son of William the Conqueror. This was replaced by a stone keep in the reign of Henry II, and Henry III had the curtain wall and gate-house built around 1250. The castle remained in royal custody until 1618, by when it was partly ruinous.

The Black Gate, still resolutely medieval but renovated into a
private dwelling in the early seventeenth century.

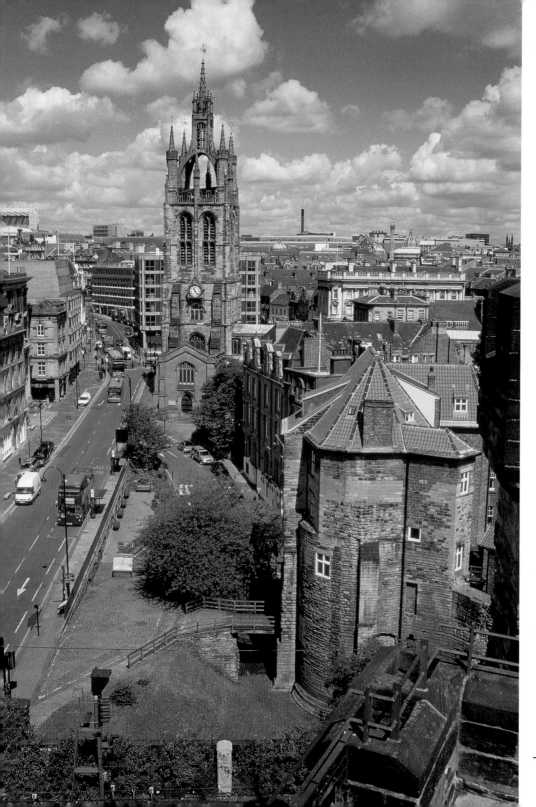

A view from a turret of the Castle Keep, over the Black Gate and St Nicholas' Cathedral, up Nicholas Street and the Groat Market. The cathedral is Early English, dating to around 1350, though the original church was at least Norman. The distinctive lantern tower was added around 1400.

People sometimes wonder how the pigeons know when
it is time to gather at the city's pavement cafés.

Queen Victoria,
dozing in St Nicholas' Square.

A demonic rabbit crouches above a doorway into Cathedral Buildings, at Amen Corner, close to the site of Thomas Bewick's workshop at the back of St Nicholas' Cathedral.

St John's Church on Grainger Street, one of the prettiest and most compact of the city's medieval churches.

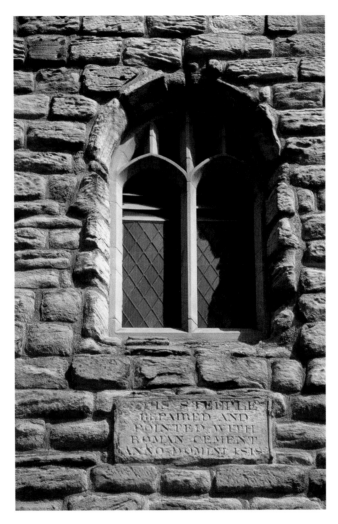

Detail from the tower of St John's Church –
'repaired and pointed with Roman cement'.

St Andrew's Church on Newgate Street, hemmed in on all sides by tall dark buildings but still looking bright and sunny on a spring morning. The church is one of the oldest in the city, dating back to the twelfth century.

St Mary's Church, standing high and proud on the Gateshead side of the Tyne, but now overshadowed by a new next-door neighbour, the Sage. The church building houses Gateshead Tourist Information Centre and a visitor centre.

The Bishop's House – East Denton Hall – on the West Road. An impressive Elizabethan mansion, built in the reign of James I and (according to local legend) haunted by a particularly nasty ghost.

Arrow-slit window in the Hebden Tower of the Town
Walls. The walls were built in the fourteenth century
and were never breached. They became redundant
as Newcastle expanded, but were brought back into
fighting order for the Jacobite Rebellion and the
Napoleonic Wars.

Secret stonework and suspended
doorways at the Black Gate.

Medieval to modern: a fragment of the Town Walls and a view of All Saints.
The rest of the scene, from City Road to the river, is dominated by building sites, steel girders and concrete.

A corner of the West Walls, next to Stowell Street.

The Sallyport Gate, last of the surviving town gateways, positioned where the City Walls cross the line of Hadrian's Wall.
The Sallyport was rebuilt in 1716 by the Company of Ships' Carpenters to serve as their meeting-hall.
It is now a popular loafing place for pigeons.

Tucked away in the suburbs, off Broomridge Avenue in Benwell, is a little Roman temple dedicated to *Antenociticus*. Although close to Hadrian's Wall and the site of a Roman fort, there is nothing visible nearby to tell you this was a thriving settlement in the early days of the occupation.

Holy Jesus Hospital, a sort of Renaissance-style almshouse, built around 1681 for poor freemen. The site had previously been an Augustinian Friary, then a meeting place for Henry VIII's 'Council of the North'. It is now an urban office of the National Trust.

Newcastle Opera House, one of the most imposing and valued of music venues
(for all sorts of music), but with a troubled history and often under new management.

Blandford House, the old CWS warehouse on Blandford Square, which now houses the Discovery Museum.
A good example of a traditional building put to contemporary use – in this case as a science museum.
Exhibits tell the story of Newcastle's industrial heritage and the dramatic discoveries by its pioneers.
The prize exhibit is the *Turbinia*, the world's first turbine-powered ship.

Kings Walk and the gateway to the University Quadrangle. Newcastle is home to two universities – Newcastle and Northumbria – and the walkways and cafes are often awash with young people clutching writing pads and bottles of mineral water.

In the Quadrangle of the University of Newcastle. A few yards away are the entrances to the Hutton Gallery and the Museum of Antiquities – both worth a visit, but not on the same day.

Eldon Square, a haven of peace on a busy shopping day. Each afternoon a corner of the square
becomes a meeting place for Goths – gentle people who like to dress up as scary monsters.
In the distance is the Grey Monument, at the cusp of 'Classical Newcastle'.

South-west over the city from the top of the Grey Monument, across Eldon Square to St James' Park.
The elaborate *art nouveau* building in the foreground is Emerson Chambers, built in 1904 and now a book-shop.

'Classical Newcastle', the core of the city now known as Grainger Town, was created around the 1830s by a group of architects and entrepreneurs led by Richard Grainger and John Dobson. Grey Street is a typically grand example of their work and the Theatre Royal is one of its most dramatic buildings. The theatre opened in 1858 with a performance of *The Merchant of Venice*. Shakespeare is still part of the repertoire, courtesy of the Royal Shakespeare Company.

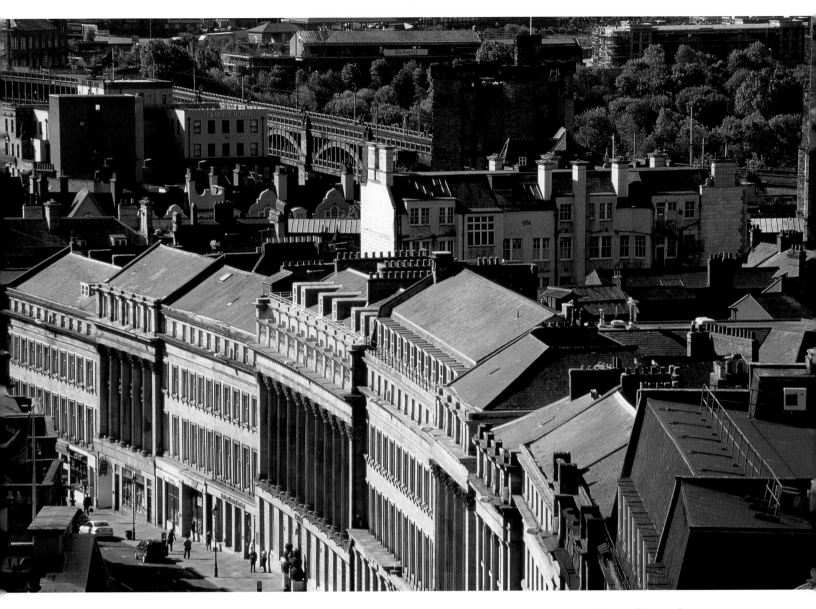

Grey Street from the Grey Monument. A graceful curve of warm sandstone façades and Corinthian columns.

The Grey Monument, Monument Metro Station and Monument Mall. The raised 'stage' at the foot of the column
is often used for live music events and speeches, and as the rallying point for protest marches:
a mixture of Hyde Park and Trafalgar Square.

Earl Grey was a local hero turned Prime Minister, commemorated here not for his taste in tea but for his Reform Bill of 1832. The statue was the work of Edward Baily, who also created Nelson on his column in Trafalgar Square.

Jeweller's Shop clock on the corner of Pilgrim Street.
The art deco figure is known as the Brazen Hussy.

The 1960s, the era of T. Dan Smith, left several scars but few enduring landmarks in Newcastle. The Civic Centre, in the Haymarket, is an exception. The distinctive tower is crowned with a circle of twelve seahorse heads.

Vane Park in Jesmond: exclusive flats
in one of the best parts of town.

Cruddas Park tower blocks from Westgate Road: not so exclusive, built in the 1960s as part of T. Dan Smith's dream of a 'City in the Sky'.

Tebay Drive, wearing white for Eastertide.

With a high student population, whole streets have a jaunty but slightly dishevelled look. The upside-down sign in a window on Falconar Street reads 'Silence, Examination in Progress'.

Bigg Market – one of the city's hot-spots, but sometimes a little seedy by daylight.

A traditional city pub, the Bee Hive, on the corner of New Bridge Street and Cloth Market. Busy at tea-time and bursting by nine.

A new venue to meet, eat and see the latest film releases: The Gate on Newgate Street.

The Central Arcade, between
Grey Street and Grainger Street.
The atmosphere is often of sepulchral
calm, despite the regular presence of
buskers (who are usually talented
students practising their instruments).

Northumberland Street, one of the busiest pedestrian thoroughfares in Newcastle, on a midsummer morning. In mid-December, when Fenwick's has its Christmas window display in full swing, it is impossible to get from one side of the street to the other without being knocked over by an over-burdened granny or a wayward Santa Claus.

Street or barrow-traders are the life and soul of any city.
Albert Sayer's family has been in the business for three centuries
and his stall on Northumberland Street always does brisk business.
He had been up at four to collect the first cherries of the season.

Breakfast on Melbourne Street...

...and on Bigg Market.

The past, present and future of your life, told by a Welsh gypsy on Bigg Market.

Stowell Street in Chinatown: vibrant and colourful. The restaurants back onto a well-preserved section of the Town Walls.

Evening rush-hour on Mosley Street.

Stay in the right lane. An evening saunter from Barras Bridge to the Haymarket.

Concrete jumble. The Central Motorway, with pedestrian fly-overs
and footbridges, looks very 1960s but works effectively.

North from Gateshead to Newcastle, through an iron forest.

St James' Park football stadium, the home of Newcastle United FC, dominates the skyline
just as the team is the main topic of conversation in the streets and pubs.

The quieter side of St James' Park: mute swans in Leazes Park.

Ten minutes to kick off. The crowd arrives late at St James' Park, but is always full of good humour (and beer). The police horses are trained to look bored.

The Gallowgate crowd streaming in for the last game of the season.

Cemeteries are sometimes austere and cold, sometimes leafy and mysterious. Newcastle has both kinds. This is the old Westgate Road Cemetery, definitely one of the leafy kind. In the distance is St Matthew's Church in Summerhill.

All Saints' Cemetery – a peaceful place set alongside the busy Jesmond Road.
Angels with anchors often decorate the graves of shipbuilders and seafarers.

The Sailors' Bethel, above Sandgate and the Quayside. This sailors' chapel was built in 1877 (to replace an older structure), and like many of Newcastle's historic buildings, it is now used as offices.

One of the more colourful neighbourhoods: Belle Grove Terrace at Castle Leazes.
Laburnum is one of the commonest garden shrubs in the city and suburbs.

Ragwort often grows where land is neglected
and in need of a splash of colour, as here at
Pipewellgate in Gateshead.

Almond blossom, close to the Royal Grammar School at Eslington Road.

Formal borders and the Almond Pavillion: civic pride on show at Saltwell Park in Gateshead.

First rose: early June in Saltwell Park.

Sunday morning at Saltwell Park: kids of all ages along the west shore of the lake.

Still waters in the heart of the city, at Leazes Park.
The lake has been stocked with some impressive and elusive fish, especially carp.

Deep wooded valleys, or 'denes',
are characteristic of the North East.
Over the years, most in Newcastle
have been smoothed out and built
over, but a few have survived and
are now treasured as green spaces.
This is Jesmond Dene in early June.

Pets' Corner in Jesmond Dene, where local people get to know
local goats, chickens and other characters.

Dappled sunshine in a corner of Leazes Park. Quiet oases are always close at hand,
even though the main shopping malls are only five minutes away.

Nuns Moor, once owned by the Church, is one of Newcastle's extensive green spaces,
managed by the City Council with the support of local residents.

The Ouse Burn, looking north from Byker Bank. This area of the city, once known for its innovative craft industries, is now being revitalised as a creative business area.

Cruddas Park from Westgate Road Cemetery: another area destined for change.

Having driven into the city via the radial dual carriageway, it comes as a surprise to find yourself
passing herds of cattle in the wide pastures of Town Moor and Nuns Moor (pictured here).
The cattle often gather in this shady avenue near Cow Hill.

Each summer, Town Moor hosts The Hoppings, billed as the biggest travelling fair in Europe.
It began as a temperance festival in 1882.

Helter Skelter at The Hoppings:
a traditional pleasure with a useful
message: don't forget your mat –
a paradigm for life.

Staff are always wanted for the Ghost Train.

Busy parts of town sometimes have a deceptive rural charm. On the slip-road to Claremont Road, overlooking the A167.

The Western Bypass (A1) and slip-road for Gateshead and the Angel of the North.
The iconic figure is loved and loathed in equal measure by people living nearby.

A lay-by on the A167 allows easy access to visit Antony Gormley's towering Angel of the North. Standing at its foot on the grassy knoll, looking up to the shifting sky, it can seem that the Angel is a pivot around which the landscape turns.

Bold colours and a bird's-eye view north-east from the top of the Castle Keep. Artist Emma Holliday is at work on a new canvas.

Spheres, the work of Richard Cole, along the riverside near Amethyst Road. Across the Tyne are Dunston Coal Staithes.

Waiting for a bus at Gateshead Interchange. A public work of art by
Danny Lane called Opening Line runs between the platforms.

Unreal city: Millennium and Sage, like a futuristic Venice.

Newcastle Law Courts on the Quayside.
The Dumfries sandstone glows salmon-pink in the evening sunlight.

Clubs, bars and restaurants with strange-sounding names fill the city's nooks and crannies.

Steel-blue sky mirrored in the roof of The Sage at Gateshead. The new concert hall and complex will cater for all kinds of music, from Northern sinfonia to Folkworks.

The Baltic: a big space for big ideas in art. The Centre for Contemporary Arts houses four main galleries.
There are no permanent exhibitions: everything changes.

Crossing the Millennium Bridge, from Gateshead to Newcastle. The half-hidden golden globe on the far side marks the Swirle Pavillion, part sculpture, part folly. The Promenade, Keelman Square and Sandgate all feature public art.

The Co-operative Society Warehouse on the Quayside is probably the oldest ferro-concrete building in the country.
It suits its location well and looks surprisingly comfortable among more modern Quayside architecture.

Like other grand buildings, the Co-op warehouse has kept its face but changed its purpose.
It is now the Malmaison Hotel.

Ex-smokers of a certain age will recognise the Wills Cigarette Factory, on the Coast Road (A1058).
An image of it appeared for many years on packets of Woodbine cigarettes.

W.D and H.O. Wills opened their Newcastle factory, an art deco icon, in the late 1940s and it closed in 1986. After years of dereliction, the building was transformed into a residential block with 114 apartments.

Crossing the King Edward's Bridge. From a window seat, looking east,
the view from this train will be nothing less than spectacular.

Newcastle Central Station: a curve of the track away from the King Edward's Bridge, to the lower left.
The Edinburgh to London train is pulling out of the station.

The Central Station was built by John Dobson around 1850, but his monumental designs for the portico had to be scaled down and it was not ready until 1865.

The eye-catching curves of the Central Station's roof are the result of an innovative design using curved malleable iron principals and wrought-iron ties. Even so, the station often functions as a wind tunnel: standing waiting for a late or cancelled train can be a chilly experience.

North-east from Whickham Thorns, across the Western Bypass and the Tyne to the heart of the city.

Glorious colours are not just reserved for important buildings.
This gas-holder (one of a rare breed) catches the eye in an
otherwise drab block of land south of Scotswood Road.

The Laing Art Gallery was built as an extension to the City Library in 1884.
The library has since been demolished to make way for John Dobson Street, but the famous
gallery remains. Ivy-framed masterpieces now decorate the blank wall facing the road.

Public art can be functional, as in the Blue Carpet on the square in front of the Laing Art Gallery. The tiles are made of blue glass bound in resin, and at its edges, the 'carpet' curves and rides up against benches and bollards.

The Tuxedo Princess. A floating night-club moored on the Gateshead side of the river, beneath the Tyne Bridge.

The Life Science Centre, in Times Square, runs events and exhibitions explaining the origins of life.
The emphasis is on making science fun for young people.

Late evening on Wesgate Road. The circle of light on Nexus House is a piece of public art by Ron Hasleden.
Above it is a tower with red neon lights, displaying world news, times and temperatures.

Opposite Nexus House, looking down Westgate Road from the corner of Blenheim Street. Renewal is an on-going process.

The West Road at Denton – running straight and true into the city. The buildings and pavement on the right-hand side of the road overlie the foundations of Hadrian's Wall. An exposed fragment of the Wall survives at the filling station.

The glory of Classical Newcastle:
from Grey Street to the Castle Keep
and High Level Bridge.

Tyne Bridge by night. Time to party.